Ten Poems
for a Picnic

ex libris

Candlestick Press

Published by:
Candlestick Press,
Diversity House, 72 Nottingham Road, Arnold, Nottingham UK NG5 6LF
www.candlestickpress.co.uk

Design and typesetting by Diversity Creative Marketing Solutions Ltd.,
www.diversity.agency

Printed by Ratcliff & Roper Print Group, Nottinghamshire, UK

Selection and Introduction © Jacqueline Gabbitas, 2018

Cover illustration © GoodStudio/Shutterstock

Candlestick Press monogram © Barbara Shaw, 2008

© Candlestick Press, 2018

ISBN 978 1 907598 65 4

Acknowledgements:

The poems in this pamphlet are reprinted from the following books, all by
permission of the publishers listed unless stated otherwise. Every effort has
been made to trace the copyright holders of the poems published in this book.
The editor and publisher apologise if any material has been included without
permission or without the appropriate acknowledgement, and would be glad to be
told of anyone who has not been consulted. Thanks are due to all the copyright
holders cited below for their kind permission:

Wayne Burrows, *The Apple Sequence* (Orchard Editions, 2011) by kind
permission of the author.

Jacqueline Gabbitas, poem first published in this anthology.

Katherine Gallagher, *Tigers on the Silk Road* (Arc Publications, 2000),
© Katherine Gallagher, 2000, reprinted by permission of Arc Publications and
the author.

Jeremy Hooker, *Adamah* (Enitharmon, 2002).

Mimi Khalvati, *The Meanest Flower* (Carcanet Press, 2007).

Edwin Morgan, *Collected Poems* (Carcanet Press, 1997).

Frank O'Hara, *The Collected Poems of Frank O'Hara* (Alfred A. Knopf, 1999),
copyright © 1971 by Maureen Granville-Smith, Administratrix of the Estate of
Frank O'Hara, copyright renewed 1999 by Maureen O'Hara Granville-Smith and
Donald Allen. Used by permission of Alfred A. Knopf, an imprint of the Knopf
Doubleday Publishing Group, a division of Penguin Random House LLC. All
rights reserved.

Peter Phillips, *Wide Skies, Salt and Best Bitter* (Hearing Eye, 2005) by kind
permission of the author.

Edna St. Vincent Millay, *Collected Poems* (Carcanet Press; HarperCollins, 2011).

All permissions cleared courtesy of Swift Permissions
(swiftpermissions@gmail.com)

Where poets are no longer living, their dates are given.

Introduction

When I started putting this compilation together there was snow on the ground and Christmas had not long past, so thinking about sitting outside to eat, drink and laugh with friends seemed a strange endeavour. But it was surprisingly easy – looking out at the snow brought up cherished memories of sitting on top of Calton Hill in Edinburgh on New Year's Day eating fruit cake and drinking brandy-laced coffee from our new flask (which is now very old and still with us). This journey of memories took me to other picnics – solar eclipses on Parliament Hill, Japanese-style cherry blossom festivals, packed lunches on school trips, and good old-fashioned checker-cloth picnic basket days.

As well as tasty food, these feasts all had one thing in common – good company. So, when I came to think about the poems for this anthology, I found myself choosing ones that not only celebrated picnics, food and drink, but people too. I was also surprised by how many poems I like about tea (but that Candlestick pamphlet's already been published so I had to think about other drinks!)

Many of the poems here sing of the lyric moment – a human moment, where the pouring of tea, drinking a can of Coke, chatting while blackberry picking, sharing apples and pears with a stranger, is an act of love. Poems here, such as Gertrude Stein's 'Custard', revel in the sounds and joy of their subjects, or, like Wayne Burrow's 'The Orchard Reborn', cast an intimate eye over history, or like Mimi Khalvati's 'Ghazal', celebrate the world in which we live and the poetry it gives us.

This compilation is made of poems I'd love to read out loud to someone or have read to me at a picnic. It means I don't have to pack an extra bag just for all the books! All I need is my little pamphlet, a flask of wine (or tea) and thou beside me.

Jacqueline Gabbitas

Recuerdo

We were very tired, we were very merry –
We had gone back and forth all night on the ferry.
It was bare and bright, and smelled like a stable –
But we looked into a fire, we leaned across a table,
We lay on a hill-top underneath the moon;
And the whistles kept blowing, and the dawn came soon.

We were very tired, we were very merry –
We had gone back and forth all night on the ferry;
And you ate an apple, and I ate a pear,
From a dozen of each we had bought somewhere;
And the sky went wan, and the wind came cold,
And the sun rose dripping, a bucketful of gold.

We were very tired, we were very merry,
We had gone back and forth all night on the ferry.
We hailed, "Good morrow, mother!" to a shawl-covered head,
And bought a morning paper, which neither of us read;
And she wept, "God bless you!" for the apples and pears,
And we gave her all our money but our subway fares.

Edna St. Vincent Millay (1892 – 1950)

(iii) The Orchard Reborn (A Boy Had Planted a Young Tree)

(after Aleksiej Pysin, Mahileu, Byelorussia, 1950)

A boy had planted a young tree,
his first tree, an apple tree placed, by this boy,
in a dark loam that would ease its roots
on their journey to a water-source.
When that boy wiped earth from his hands,
saw other trees, towering high,
he hoped his sapling might catch up soon,
bring apples in autumn, green in spring,
and, seeing how vast the full sky was,
he wished for boughs to fill it,
growth to begin and climb the air
until the clouds jostled in his tree's canopy.
He asked: *Grow tree. Grow up and thrive,*
then turned to go. He didn't hear
the roots say *yes*, the leaves grasp a light breeze
or send their message to the river oaks:
didn't notice by what small degree
the world had grown fairer when he walked away.
A boy had planted a young tree.

Wayne Burrows

Custard

Custard is this. It has aches, aches when. Not to be. Not to be narrowly. This makes a whole little hill.

It is better than a little thing that has mellow real mellow. It is better than lakes whole lakes, it is better than seeding.

Gertrude Stein (1874 – 1946)

Cakes at Sheringham Park

Around every corner flash fires of light,
shadows of colour printed on paths.

But I don't smell the rhododendrons,
their huge bell flowers tolling in the breeze.

What I see are strawberry and raspberry tarts,
apricot flans and creamy cheesecake.

I breathe in, taste the colours,
go in search of a cup of tea.

Peter Phillips

Ghazal

after Hafez

However large earth's garden, mine's enough.
One rose and the shade of a vine's enough.

I don't want more wealth, I don't need more dross.
The grape has its bloom and it shines enough.

Why ask for the moon? The moon's in your cup,
a beggar, a tramp, for whom wine's enough.

Look at the stream as it winds out of sight.
One glance, one glimpse of a chine's enough.

Like the sun in bazaars, streaming in shafts,
any slant on the grand design's enough.

When you're here, my love, what more could I want?
Just mentioning love in a line's enough.

Heaven can wait. To have found, heaven knows,
a bed and a roof so divine's enough.

I've no grounds for complaint. As Hafez says,
isn't a ghazal that he signs enough?

Mimi Khalvati

Hanami, Hai
(for Martin)

Our Walthamstow park –
blossom clouding the trees just
like Shinjiku Park.

Not pink *sakura*,
but white may blossom, too soon
for plum or apple.

Branches full, eager
to shout out a big fat yes!
for you to come home.

You say you're safe and
though the flight over was bad,
the earthquakes less so.

And Fukushima,
a new word for sadness, hangs
like cherry blossom.

I sit here beneath
English hawthorns offering
soup to their *kami*.

And time, yes, is stretched.
Your *hanami* will happen
tomorrow, mine now.

You'll sit there beneath
sakura trees in a crowd
of strangers and friends.

Parties stake their claim
under the canopies with
bōsui shūto.

I didn't need to
claim my tree in Walthamstow.
I call your mobile.

Happy Hanami!
Half asleep you laugh, then ask:
what are you eating?

Onigiri, rice,
miso shiru, gyoza,
inari sushi.

Good, you say to me,
save some room for the *sake*.
I'm bringing it home.

Jacqueline Gabbitas

Knebworth Park

A cave of air softens,
hovers over our heads.
We've waited all year for this:
the March lull, the park
almost tourist-free.

Put your ear
to this unsaddled soil,
sound out the mating-calls
of otters, rabbits, voles;
hear horses' hoofbeats
pound nearer-far.

I have made an altar of calm
among these ageing oaks,
lines of stiff-backed trees.

Our walk circles the ancient house,
grounds set off by daffodils.
A five-year-old sings a nursery rhyme,
wanting to pat sheep. Their beady eyes
distract, promising only puzzles.

We call ourselves comfortable explorers,
notice a wine-glass left among the ferns.
A squirrel skids into wintry hiding.
As the light fades, we study
each other's faces
for signs of sun.

Katherine Gallagher

Having a Coke With You

is even more fun than going to San Sebastian, Irún, Hendaye, Biarritz, Bayonne
or being sick to my stomach on the Travesera de Gracia in Barcelona
partly because in your orange shirt you look like a better happier St. Sebastian
partly because of my love for you, partly because of your love for yoghurt
partly because of the fluorescent orange tulips around the birches
partly because of the secrecy our smiles take on before people and statuary
it is hard to believe when I'm with you that there can be anything as still
as solemn as unpleasantly definitive as statuary when right in front of it
in the warm New York 4 o'clock light we are drifting back and forth
between each other like a tree breathing through its spectacles

and the portrait show seems to have no faces in it at all, just paint
you suddenly wonder why in the world anyone ever did them
                                                                      I look
at you and I would rather look at you than all the portraits in the world
except possibly for the *Polish Rider* occasionally and anyway it's in the Frick
which thank heavens you haven't gone to yet so we can go together the first time
and the fact that you move so beautifully more or less takes care of Futurism
just as at home I never think of the *Nude Descending a Staircase* or
at a rehearsal a single drawing of Leonardo or Michelangelo that used to wow me
and what good does all the research of the Impressionists do them
when they never got the right person to stand near the tree when the sun sank
or for that matter Marino Marini when he didn't pick the rider as carefully
as the horse
                     it seems they were all cheated of some marvellous experience
which is not going to go wasted on me which is why I'm telling you about it

Frank O'Hara (1926 – 1966)

Blackberrying: A Conversation Piece

Whether birds feel joy in their flight
Whether one's lifework might be something no one wants
Whether one will end up living in a cardboard box
Whether love is an element like air or fire
Such are the questions on their purple tongues.

Jeremy Hooker

The Picnic

In a little rainy mist of white and grey
we sat under an old tree,
drank tea toasts to the powdery mountain,
undrunk got merry, played catch
with the empty flask, on the pine needles
came down to where it rolled stealthily away –

you lay
with one arm in the rain, laughing
shaking only your wet hair
loose against the grass, in that enchanted place
of tea, with curtains of a summer rain
dropped round us, for a rainy day.

Edwin Morgan (1920 – 2010)